Amy,
    May your family
always have love
and joy!
    Blessings,
        Nancy Beck

PILLOW TALK

Loving affirmations to encourage and guide your children

Nancy Beck, BSN, RN

- Illustrations by -
Sarah Minor

beck Global Publishing

Ashland, MO
www.beckglobalpublishing.com

Published and distributed in the United States by Beck Global Publishing, Inc.:
www.beckglobalpublishing.com

Editorial supervision: Denise Vultee, Ph.D., dmvultee@gmail.com; Linda Gentry,
lindagentry@hypnosismo.com
Book cover illustrator: Sarah Minor, www.sarahminor.com
Book illustrator and designer: Sarah Minor, www.sarahminor.com
Photograph of author by Carl Neitzert, Creative Photo, www.CPportraits.com
Printed by Walsworth Publishing Company, Marceline, MO

Library of Congress Control Number: 2008903411

ISBN 13: 978-0-9816942-0-7
ISBN 10: 0-9816942-0-9

1st printing, April 2008
Printed in the United States of America

Dear Reader,

Hello! I have discovered such an important secret that I have to share it. That secret is the power of Pillow Talk to bring greater depths of love and connection between parents and children. I believe if every child could experience the power of Pillow Talk, the world would be a better place. The concept of Pillow Talk is simple to apply: It means giving positive affirmations to your children when they are asleep and watching them benefit from the results.

There are two parts to *Pillow Talk*. In Part One, using common topics that most families have encountered, I provide examples of how Pillow Talk has helped my own family. My favorite example is the time when my nearly two-year-old daughter started to use the words "I love you" after her first experience with Pillow Talk.

In Part Two, I will give you directions so you can start using your own Pillow Talk.

I dedicate this book to my children. For the sake of their privacy, I am using the names "Michael" and "Sarah."

Many Blessings,
Nancy

THANK YOU!

I want to thank the following people: Gerald Kein for his part in bringing this secret into my life; Linda Gentry, my technical editor, much of whose wisdom has helped to shape the person I am today, for kindly nudging me to make this book a reality; Denise Vultee, my copy editor; Sarah Minor, the book's designer and illustrator; Mary Kennedy, Dr. John Baird, and Gary Langston for sharing special feedback, along with numerous friends and colleagues; Dr. Douglas Beal and Lynn Ogden for taking special time to write endorsements; Linda Sypkens for her friendship; my in-laws, Don and Joan Beck, for helping with the children as needed; and a special thanks to my husband, Mark Beck, for all it takes to make a family work with all we have going on in our lives. Bless them all.

Table of Contents

Part One: My Life Examples

Part Two: Create Your Own Affirmations

Part One: My Life Examples

It is simple

We talk to our children and tell them all the things we want them to know about life. I know, I know, you do this all the time. Right? But what makes the approach described in this book different from the conversations you already have with your children is that it shows you how you can also talk to them while they are asleep; thus the title *Pillow Talk*.

This approach works because they listen. Why? Perhaps they listen because their other senses are not distracting their attention. They are not watching the TV across the room, listening to the sounds from outside, thinking about that cookie they want to have at lunch, or touching that satin trim on their favorite blanket. They are listening to you.

Using Pillow Talk has changed our lives in beautiful and profound ways. As you read the Pillow Talk topic examples in this section, you will understand what I mean.

How to read this book

For each Pillow Talk topic, I let you know what was going on in our lives, the affirmations I gave my children, and how my children responded; I then end with a personal reflection. Within the illustrations for each topic are some of the virtues each individual Pillow Talk may have to offer. You may find additional virtues within each topic based upon your personal beliefs.

After you have read a few of the topics, you may recognize a repetitive pattern in the layout. This is for your ease of use.

list many resources I have used to assist my parenting and give a brief summary of the information presented from each one. If you are not already familiar with the concepts, you may enjoy the reading list at the end of the book.

In Part Two, I explain how to create your own affirmations so that you too can use my discovery to help bring greater depths of love into your family's lives.

In this book I speak frequently of God. I am a very spiritual person. When I speak of God, it is in reference to my belief in God as the creator of the Universe. For ease of reading, when I speak of "God," insert your own thoughts of your personal beliefs and values. The intention of this book is to help you communicate with your children in a very personal way.

Instructions

Make this way of communicating with your child incredibly loving and nurturing. I stroke my children's hair and face as I start the affirmations; my voice starts out quiet and soft; and by the time I get to the sixth time I have used their names, my voice is strong and at a normal talking volume, confident and nurturing. When you use Pillow Talk, insert your child's name where appropriate, and refer to yourself by the name your child is used to hearing from you.

Stay asleep (Sarah), this is (Mommy) - very soft voice.
Stay asleep (Sarah), this is (Mommy) - soft voice.
Stay asleep (Sarah), this is (Mommy) - loving voice.
Stay asleep (Sarah), this is (Mommy) - normal voice.
Stay asleep (Sarah), this is (Mommy) - confident voice.
Stay asleep (Sarah), this is (Mommy) - nurturing voice.

LOVE

When I discovered Pillow Talk, my daughter Sarah was almost two years old. Even though she was talking, she had not used the words "I love you." She was also calling her older brother Michael by the name "Getty." Incidentally, there was a little girl named Gracie in Sarah's daycare who was just a couple months younger than Sarah, and Sarah would not let Gracie play in her pretend tea parties.

I had an underlying nagging concern that this behavior was related to my work schedule. When my children were very young, I worried that they might not even be aware that I was really at home every night. As a critical care nurse, I regularly worked shifts that were up to 13-14 hours long. Usually I left for work in the morning before my children were awake, and often I came home after they were in bed. This happened up to three times a week. When I got home, I would always go into their room and give them a kiss and tell them, "I love you," whether they were awake or not.

I then started using Pillow Talk, and I now use this Love Affirmation as the foundation for all my future affirmations.

This is how I begin each Pillow Talk affirmation:

Stay asleep (Sarah), this is (Mommy).
Stay asleep (Sarah), this is (Mommy).

Stay asleep (Sarah), this is (Mommy).
Stay asleep (Sarah), this is (Mommy).
Stay asleep (Sarah), this is (Mommy).
Stay asleep (Sarah), this is (Mommy).
(Sarah), I love you... thank you for being in my life... I am the luckiest (mommy) in the world to have such a wonderful (daughter) as (Sarah)... my heart is filled with joy and the world is a better place because you are in it... I love you with all my heart...

I love you because... (insert the very personal, wonderful things that you see in your child).

I say different things to Sarah than to my son Michael. They are very different people, and they each have different things to offer the world. My words may vary every night depending on the day's events:

(Sarah), I love you because... you are smart... and funny... and you run like the wind... wow... you are wonderful... you amaze me...

(Michael), I love you because... you are smart... you really know how to figure things out... you are safe and take good care of yourself... I love it that you understand right from wrong...

When I talk to them like this, it reminds me of how I talked to them when I was pregnant, or when they were infants and I looked into their faces and told them all the wonderful, loving feelings I had for them. (Go ahead and be spontaneous. See Part Two for guidance rules for creating your own affirmations.) After I had been giving the above affirmation for just a week, my daughter was saying, "I love you"; she was using Michael's name; and she was inviting Gracie to play with her in tea parties.

Reflection: Our actions are usually more important than our words. Love is a large concept, and we all have different ideas about love and what it means to us. As beautiful an experience as I had with my daughter Sarah, when I think of the love I have for my children, my mind has to step in for a minute and give guidance to my heart. Let me explain.

My husband Mark and I learned about setting boundaries in a class based on Dr. Becky Bailey's strategies, called "Conscious Discipline."

Dr. Bailey discusses the need for setting solid boundaries to make our children feel safe. When children feel safe, they are best able to reach their full potential as thinking human beings, knowing that actions have consequences. As a parent, that is what I want for my children: that they grow up as loving, independent, thinking, and contributing individuals. In class, we were given the opportunity to practice giving our children acceptable choices instead of using time-outs or physical discipline.

So, to keep building on this idea, our children challenge our love as parents in their actions. This is called "testing boundaries." When we see this reaction in young children, we often call it a tantrum. In teenagers, we see rebellious behavior; there is not much difference between the two. So our willingness to keep firm boundaries is a demonstration of our love as parents.

Many of us instinctually want to give in to our children's requests. It may seem like a good solution to the short-term problem: the crying. It may seem as if our children really want whatever they are asking for, so if we give in to their tantrums, they will know how much we love them. However, when we as parents set boundaries, we need to make them very solid, so when young children test them, they can feel safe knowing we are consistent. It is the consistency they thrive on developmentally. And (this was a new concept for me), in that moment of the tantrum, the child really is not expecting to receive what they requested; they are checking to see how strongly we are able to set our boundaries as parents. When you keep to your instincts about the situation, even when it is against the child's will, you are creating a feeling of safety. In that feeling of safety, one of your children's greatest needs is being met, and they are better able to experience the depths of your love. Otherwise, their minds are in a state of confusion, and that confusion can slow emotional development.

This is an important concept to learn and understand. After I learned it, my parenting became easier. From the class I took based on Dr. Bailey's book, my role as a parent became more clearly defined.

As a parent, I see it as my responsibility to provide a loving and safe environment for my children at all times. I set boundaries, and I attempt to recognize when my children are testing them. My goal is not to be reactive but to be proactive by setting structure. For example, if I make clear to my children before we enter a restaurant what sort of behavior I expect from them and what the consequences of unexpected behavior will be, I am being *proactive*, and they are much more likely to behave in the ways I expect from them. If, instead, I wait until they engage in unacceptable behavior in the restaurant, then respond with an unplanned and unexpected consequence, I am being *reactive*, and we are all upset.

WALKING IN FRONT OF CARS

Sarah was walking right before she was ten months old. She loves her independence and exploring her world. At daycare she had been pushing and wiggling herself out of my arms and then running down the driveway toward the street. As you know, this can make your heart stop. I could not seem to find the right discipline to keep her from repeating this unsafe behavior over and over and over. She seemed to love the chase that always ensued when she managed to break free. She was almost two when I learned about Pillow Talk, so I thought it would be exciting to see what I could do to help. I gave her the following affirmation:

Stay asleep (Sarah), this is (Mommy).
Stay asleep (Sarah), this is (Mommy).
Stay asleep (Sarah), this is (Mommy).
Stay asleep (Sarah), this is (Mommy).
Stay asleep (Sarah), this is (Mommy).
Stay asleep (Sarah), this is (Mommy).

(Sarah), I love you... thank you for being in my life... I am the luckiest (mommy) in the world to have such a wonderful (daughter) as (Sarah)... my

heart is filled with joy and the
world is a better
place because you
are in it... I love you
with all my heart...

(Sarah),... driveways
and parking lots can
be dangerous... there
are big cars that can
hurt you... no one wants
to hurt you... you are
small and move as fast
as the wind... sometimes
the person driving the car
cannot see you... and you
might accidentally get hurt...
you need to let (Mommy,
Daddy, or whoever is with
you) hold your hand or carry
you when you are around
cars... we want to keep you
safe... we love you... you are very
important to us... so when you are
around cars... you let us carry
you or hold your hand... we love you
and want to keep you safe.

Before this Pillow Talk, I had to carry her with one arm over her shoulder and the other arm between her legs. Sarah responded well to this affirmation and allowed me to carry her to her car seat in a normal on-the-hip hold. We definitely had no more chase scenes. What a blessing for both of us.

Reflection: When I am talking to my children about safety issues, I focus on keeping them safe because they are loved. I will discuss why a particular action or situation may be dangerous. However, I do not want to create fear, but rather an awareness of how to stay safe. I used this tactic in the above Pillow Talk.

love

serenity

encouragement

HEALTH

As a nurse and a mother, I want my children to have healthy lives. I came up with the following affirmation. Perhaps it will have long-term effects.

Stay asleep (Michael), this is (Mommy).
Stay asleep (Michael), this is (Mommy).
Stay asleep (Michael), this is (Mommy).
Stay asleep (Michael), this is (Mommy).
Stay asleep (Michael), this is (Mommy).
Stay asleep (Michael), this is (Mommy).

(Michael), I love you... thank you for being in my life... I am the luckiest (mommy) in the world to have such a wonderful (son) as (Michael)... my heart is filled with joy and the world is a better place because you are in it... I love you with all my heart...

(Michael), by eating healthy foods and drinking healthy, life-giving water... you keep your body strong and healthy... you only put things into your body that keep your body healthy... you keep your body healthy and strong by only putting healthy things into your body.

This was a very effective affirmation. Both Sarah and Michael understood quite naturally what healthy foods were.

About three weeks after I started using this Pillow Talk, I was telling my husband, Mark, about the affirmation. He was not aware I was giving the kids affirmations of good health. He then chuckled and said, "That explains it." He said he was taking the kids to school, and he had stopped for donuts and chocolate milk. (I learned on that day it had been a morning tradition for them for quite some time.) Both of the kids started fussing at him about his choices, telling him how bad the donuts and chocolate milk are for all of them. He told them they did not have to have any, and he would keep it all to himself. As much as they knew it was unhealthy, they wanted the donuts and chocolate milk. They persuaded Mark to go ahead and let them have them.

My hindsight recommendation to my husband was if he had thrown the food away, the kids would have been satisfied. Unfortunately, my husband's sugar addiction made this too big a challenge.

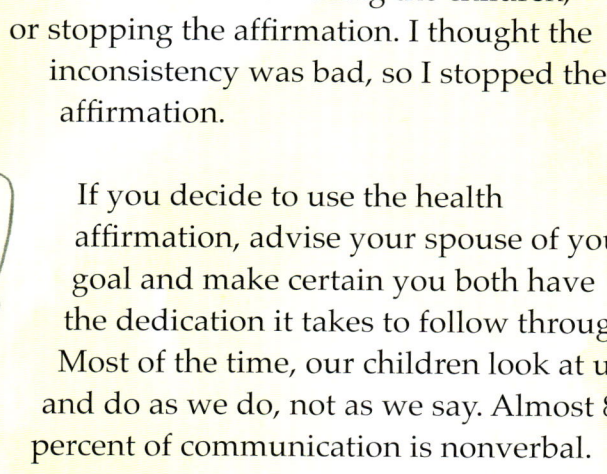

Reflection: I had a choice of continuing the affirmation and confusing the children, or stopping the affirmation. I thought the inconsistency was bad, so I stopped the affirmation.

If you decide to use the health affirmation, advise your spouse of your goal and make certain you both have the dedication it takes to follow through. Most of the time, our children look at us and do as we do, not as we say. Almost 80 percent of communication is nonverbal.

nourishment

fitness

health

HEALING

Both of our children love to be active, and they get the usual cuts and bruises children get. In my work as a nurse, I know how important attitude is for healing the body. I want both of my children to realize how strong their bodies are so they can take advantage of God's creation and the body's natural ability to heal.

Stay asleep (Sarah), this is (Mommy).
Stay asleep (Sarah), this is (Mommy).
Stay asleep (Sarah), this is (Mommy).
Stay asleep (Sarah), this is (Mommy).
Stay asleep (Sarah), this is (Mommy).
Stay asleep (Sarah), this is (Mommy).

(Sarah), I love you... thank you for being in my life... I am the luckiest (mommy) in the world to have such a wonderful (daughter) as (Sarah)... my heart is filled with joy and the world is a better place because you are in it... I love you with all my heart...

(Sarah), your body is perfectly designed by (God)... your body is strong and healthy... you heal quickly... (God) created you to be strong and healthy and to heal quickly... you have a strong and healthy body and it heals quickly.

At about the age of three, after taking a tumble, Sarah stood up quickly and said, "I am okay...

my body is strong and healthy." When either of my children get a cut, I like to point out to them their cut is healing quickly, and we look at it getting smaller each day.

Reflection: It is important to help our children focus on how well the body is working and to be thankful for their health. If your children do not often have good health, on the days or even moments when their bodies are working well, have them bless the good health. Take advantage of the good health moment by doing something they want. Stay positive and upbeat, and really focus on the desired outcomes, not on the events or illness that may be affecting them.

Napoleon Hill discusses the advantages of a positive mental attitude in his book *Think and Grow Rich*.

faith

empowerment

healing

faith

trust

empowerment

TEETH PULLED

Sarah has been independent from the start. One day when she was nearly two, I was working in the kitchen when I heard Sarah crying from the next room, where she and Michael were playing. I checked on her and discovered she had hurt her mouth from a fall, but there was no sign of an injury. I comforted her. The next morning I discovered part of her lower front tooth was missing; it had fallen out in her sleep. I took her to see her pediatric dentist; at that time there was nothing more to do. As she turned three, however, she suddenly developed an abscess at the root of the tooth. I took her to the dentist again and was told the tooth would have to be removed. The dentist said she would try extracting it in the office, but if Sarah would not cooperate it might have to be removed in the hospital under anesthesia. I decided use Pillow Talk and called the office a few days before the scheduled procedure to get step-by-step instructions. This is what I said:

Stay asleep (Sarah), this is (Mommy).
Stay asleep (Sarah), this is (Mommy).
Stay asleep (Sarah), this is (Mommy).
Stay asleep (Sarah), this is (Mommy).
Stay asleep (Sarah), this is (Mommy).
Stay asleep (Sarah), this is (Mommy).

(Sarah), I love you... thank you for being in my life... I am the luckiest (mommy) in the world to have such a wonderful (daughter) as (Sarah)... my heart is filled with joy and the world is a better place because you are in it... I love you with all my heart...

(Sarah), you are going to go to see (Dr. Lori) to have your tooth pulled... (Dr. Lori) says that to keep you healthy your tooth needs to be taken out... (Dr. Lori) will be very careful and will keep you safe... this is what is going to happen... I will be with you... we are going to go to (Dr. Lori's) office and you will sit in a special chair... (Dr. Lori) is going to look at your tooth with a special instrument that will have a little point on it... but she will be very careful and not hurt you... then she is going to put a mask over your face and give you happy air so you don't feel much as she works on your tooth... then she is going to put a special medicine on a piece of cotton and hold it on your gum so you do not feel much of anything... after the medicine is working you won't feel much of anything... then she will give you a small shot... but you won't feel much... because (Dr. Lori) is going to be very careful... she will take your tooth out and you won't feel much of anything... taking this tooth out will help keep your body healthy... it will be easy for you... I will be right there... and when it is over you don't need to bleed... you are at the dentist's office and it is all sterile... so you don't need to bleed... I love you... you are amazing.

I used this Pillow Talk two nights in a row prior to Sarah's appointment. She did amazingly well. She walked in and sat down with great confidence. She was so brave through her whole appointment. She gave one small whimper for a moment when she saw the needle, but she sat still and behaved very well. When they were done, they put a cotton all where her tooth had been and told her to keep it there tight. She dropped it accidentally when she got up out of her hair, but there was only a speck of blood on it, and she had absolutely no other bleeding.

Reflection: My experience as a nurse has been if you tell patients what to expect, they have the skills to deal with the situation. It is important to be upfront and honest with our children. However, they do not need to know everything in the detail that we know. Use words your children can understand, and avoid surprises that might upset them. By doing these things, you are more likely to keep their trust.

Bugs

When Sarah was about three years old, a wasp stung her on her foot. I swooped her up in my arms and shook her foot, thinking the wasp would fall off, but when it didn't I screamed a horrible scream in my own fear for Sarah. I have to admit screaming like that dramatized the event a hundred times. I had to scrape the wasp off with a piece of paper before I stepped on it and killed it. I held Sarah and took care of the sting. To this day there is a small discolored spot on her foot where the sting happened.

Following this event, Sarah's daycare provider Amy said Sarah was nearly hysterical around bugs. Amy said Sarah was on the swing when a housefly came by, and Amy had to hold and comfort her. Sarah was jumpy and almost paranoid.

I used the following affirmation:

Stay asleep (Sarah), this is (Mommy).
Stay asleep (Sarah), this is (Mommy).
Stay asleep (Sarah), this is (Mommy).
Stay asleep (Sarah), this is (Mommy).
Stay asleep (Sarah), this is (Mommy).
Stay asleep (Sarah), this is (Mommy).

(Sarah), I love you... thank you for being in my life... I am the luckiest (mommy) in the world to

have such a wonderful (daughter) as (Sarah)... my heart is filled with joy and the world is a better place because you are in it... I love you with all my heart...

(Sarah), bugs are important to the world and our lives... (God) made all of the bugs and they are important... bugs are to be respected... you do not need to touch bugs... you do not need to kill bugs... they are

important and need to be respected... the next time you see a bug you can look at it and not touch it... most bugs will not hurt you... you can look at them without touching them and they will not hurt you.

Mark also had his own Pillow Talk he gave Sarah. Sarah was great. The very next day she saw a bug, and she ran and brought me to it and said, "Look, it's a bug." She pointed and smiled.

Reflection: I believe there are great lessons to be taught about (God's) creations. Therefore, I take advantage of the opportunities to teach my children about conservation. We have since bought a bug-catcher. It has a long handle, a collection area, and a sliding bottom. We catch bugs and release them outside.

respect

love

creation

PROTECTION

There is nothing unusual about children being afraid at night-time. Michael and Sarah share the same bedroom. They both were having difficulty at night-time feeding off of each other's fears. After a conversation with my dear friend Linda Gentry, I came up with the following affirmations:

Stay asleep (Michael), this is (Mommy).
Stay asleep (Michael), this is (Mommy).
Stay asleep (Michael), this is (Mommy).
Stay asleep (Michael), this is (Mommy).
Stay asleep (Michael), this is (Mommy).
Stay asleep (Michael), this is (Mommy).

(Michael), I love you... thank you for being in my life... I am the luckiest (mommy) in the world to have such a wonderful (son) as (Michael)... my heart is filled with joy and the world is a better place because you are in it... I love you with all my heart...

(Michael), you are safe... you and (Sarah) share the same room... (Mommy and Daddy) are right across the hall... we built this safe house to raise our family... our love protects you... you can build your own protective bubble... sort of like Violet in The Incredibles... *only this bubble controls thoughts and energy... all you do is imagine a protective bubble all around you... only loving thoughts and energy can come in... all negative and harmful thoughts bounce off and leave to go far away... only loving thoughts and energy can come in... all negative and harmful thoughts bounce off and go*

far away... imagine a protective bubble all around you... only loving thoughts and energy can come in... all negative and harmful thoughts bounce off and go far away... you are safe... our love protects you.

Violet is a character from a children's movie, *The Incredibles.* She has a special power to place an invisible force field around herself and others who are next to her to keep them safe from evil forces. It took several nights of this affirmation to start making a difference. Once it started working for Michael and Sarah, going to bed at night became less frightening for them.

Reflection: It is important that we have our children in a safe environment. It is probably the second most important thing that we can offer our children, with the first being love. Taking the parenting class on "Conscious Discipline" helped us understand what it means to keep our children feeling safe, including setting consistent boundaries. If our children live in fear, they cannot function at their highest ability.

faith

love

safety

BEAUTY

As a girl, I used to get confused about society's expectation of beauty. I struggled with self-image in relation to others around me. I wanted Sarah to understand what it took me into my adulthood to realize.

I used to look at Sarah and say, "You are so beautiful." Sarah would say, "No, Mommy. I am not beautiful, Laura is beautiful." I would correct her and say, "No, Sarah, to me you are the most beautiful person I have ever met."

Stay asleep (Sarah), this is (Mommy).
Stay asleep (Sarah), this is (Mommy).
Stay asleep (Sarah), this is (Mommy).
Stay asleep (Sarah), this is (Mommy).
Stay asleep (Sarah), this is (Mommy).
Stay asleep (Sarah), this is (Mommy).

(Sarah), I love you... thank you for being in my life... I am the luckiest (mommy) in the world to have such a wonderful (daughter) as (Sarah)... my heart is filled with joy and the world is a better place because you are in it... I love you with all my heart...

(Sarah), you are so beautiful... beautiful is not what you look

like... beauty is who you are... beauty is what you do... and you are kind and loving... you are beautiful... you are lucky because you are always going to have lots of friends and make new friends easily because you are so nice and funny to be around... you are beautiful.

Mark also had his own Pillow Talk he gave Sarah. After a few nights of these affirmations, Sarah would let me tell her she was beautiful, and she would smile and agree. She now will even walk up to me and let me know she is beautiful.

Reflection: I learned from the book *The One Minute Mother* by Spencer Johnson, M.D., that an important strategy to reinforce the concept of beauty is to catch your children doing something right, give them praise and let them know that their action was beautiful, wonderful, nice, etc.

When you identify at the time of the action what it is you like, you are reinforcing your expectations. Focus n the desired behavior without mentioning the undesired ehavior. For instance, when Sarah gives Michael a piece of er candy without his having to ask for it, I give her a hug nd let her know how beautiful it is to share, and I tell her hat it makes Michael feel loved, and makes my heart happy. he beams with pride.

sharing

beauty

friendship

HAIRCUT

I have always been a frugal person. Wanting to save a few dollars, I attempted to cut my children's hair. It would take me about an hour to cut Michael's hair, and there was absolutely no getting Sarah to sit still for a haircut. I used to wait until she fell asleep and attempt to cut her hair by turning her head one way, then another, while she slept on her pillow. After going through this process several times, I decided we did not need this tension.

I have since discovered the price of a haircut is very reasonable. Michael was already willing to sit still. However, Katie, our hairdresser, was chasing Sarah, almost age two, around the shop in an attempt to catch her sitting still long enough to get the job done. I decided to attempt Pillow Talk on Sarah after our first haircut experience. This is the affirmation I now use:

Stay asleep (Sarah),
this is (Mommy).
Stay asleep
(Sarah), this is
(Mommy).
Stay asleep (Sarah),
this is (Mommy).
Stay asleep (Sarah),
this is (Mommy).
Stay asleep (Sarah), this
is (Mommy).
Stay asleep (Sarah), this is
(Mommy).

(Sarah), I love you... thank you for being in my life... I am the luckiest (mommy) in the world to have such a wonderful (daughter) as (Sarah)... my heart is filled with joy and the world is a better place because you are in it... I love you with all my heart...

(Sarah), sitting still for a haircut is important... when you sit still it makes it easier for (Katie) to cut your hair... sit still and listen to (Katie's) instructions... she will tell you what she wants you to do to get a very nice haircut... (Katie) is our friend... and she will be very safe and give you a very nice haircut... (Sarah), remember when you get a haircut it is very important to sit still and you will have a very nice haircut.

Lesson: The above haircut affirmation was my modified script. I relearned something very important about affirmations: Always keep them positive. The first time I gave Sarah the affirmation, I told her it was important to sit still, because Katie might accidentally slip with her scissors and cut her. Well, Sarah cried the minute Katie got out the scissors, she did not stop crying until Katie was done, and she was dodging the scissors as Katie went to make a cut. It was a horrible experience for all of us. That night I went to Sarah and used the Pillow Talk to tell her:

...(Katie) would never hurt you... (Katie) cuts hair all of the time... and she knows how to be safe with her scissors... and I'm sorry I told you that you might accidentally get hurt if you move... (Katie) is our friend... and she will always be safe with her scissors.

42

I repeated the same affirmation the next night, too. It was important for me to apologize to Sarah. I had given her the wrong information. As much as I want to be a great mother, I have my faults. For me it is important to take responsibility for my mistakes and move on with my new lesson learned.

The next time Sarah had her hair cut, I used the modified haircut affirmation two nights in a row prior to her appointment. Sarah did a very nice job for Katie. She sat in the chair calmly and followed Katie's instructions. I never had to use it again.

Reflection: It has been helpful for us to have one person who cuts our entire family's hair. Katie has been a trusted friend for many years.

Only (Katie) cuts your hair

A few years later it became important to add the following affirmation after Sarah at age five took the scissors to her own hair:

Stay asleep (Sarah), this is (Mommy).
Stay asleep (Sarah), this is (Mommy).
Stay asleep (Sarah), this is (Mommy).
Stay asleep (Sarah), this is (Mommy).
Stay asleep (Sarah), this is (Mommy).
Stay asleep (Sarah), this is (Mommy).

(Sarah), I love you... thank you for being in my life...
I am the luckiest (mommy) in the world to have such
a wonderful (daughter) as (Sarah)... my heart is filled
with joy and the world is a better place because you are
in it... I love you with all my heart...

(Sarah), remember... for now only (Katie) cuts your hair...
(Katie) does a very nice job cutting your hair and keeps it
looking very nice... remember... for now only (Katie) cuts
your hair... (Katie) does a very nice job cutting your hair and
keeps it looking very nice... you have such pretty hair... and
you like the way it looks... everyone would love to have hair
as pretty as yours... you are so lucky to have such beautiful
hair... some day when you are older you may decide on your
own (haircut person)... remember... for now only (Katie) cuts
your hair... because she keeps it looking so nice...

Katie listens to Sarah and cuts her hair according to Sarah's request. I may give my input about the length, but I let the two of them decide on the cut. Sarah is the one who has to look in the mirror and like what she sees, and a haircut is a great way to let her express herself.

Reflection: The child's mind may take your affirmation very literally. It is important to leave your children the freedom to make their own choices in the future. The difficult part of this affirmation is deciding how far into the future you want it to affect your child. If the affirmation does not include a clause for choosing a different haircut person later in life, a very small percentage of children may have extreme difficulty letting someone other than (Katie) cut their hair.

trust

love

patience

45

FRIENDS

Michael is a very sweet and quiet boy. At his current age, it is socially more important to him to connect with children outside of the family than it is for Sarah. When Michael was starting a new school at age five, I used the following affirmation:

Stay asleep (Michael), this is (Mommy).
Stay asleep (Michael), this is (Mommy).
Stay asleep (Michael), this is (Mommy).
Stay asleep (Michael), this is (Mommy).
Stay asleep (Michael), this is (Mommy).
Stay asleep (Michael), this is (Mommy).

(Michael), I love you... thank you for being in my life... I am the luckiest (mommy) in the world to have such a wonderful (son) as (Michael)... my heart is filled with joy and the world is a better place because you are in it... I love you with all my heart...

(Michael),... you are so lucky... you are always going to have lots of friends because you are so nice... it is easy for you to make friends because you are so nice... you treat people with respect... you use your good manners... you are funny and you make people laugh... I have seen you... when someone is sad you make them feel better... the world is a

*better place because you are in it... thank you for being
in my life... I love you with all my heart.*

Michael does make friends easily. We were fortunate
to have a wonderful Montessori school program near
where we live that nurtured Michael's personality. He
is in a public school now, and even though he remains
quiet, he still makes friends easily. His teacher says he
has a great sense of humor that everyone appreciates.

49

FRUSTRATION

Both Michael and Sarah are very smart. Michael likes to analyze things and know how they work. Once Michael started in a Montessori program at age five, new ideas were coming to him quickly. I would watch him at the table working on putting a toy together, and then he would suddenly yell and throw the toy down and start crying out of frustration.

My response would be, "If it makes you cry, then don't play with it; it's supposed to be fun." Michael did not find this amusing or helpful. So I came up with the following affirmation:

Stay asleep (Michael), this is (Mommy).
Stay asleep (Michael), this is (Mommy).
Stay asleep (Michael), this is (Mommy).
Stay asleep (Michael), this is (Mommy).
Stay asleep (Michael), this is (Mommy).
Stay asleep (Michael), this is (Mommy).

(Michael), I love you... thank you for being in my life...
I am the luckiest (mommy) in the world to have such a
wonderful (son) as (Michael)... my heart is filled with joy
and the world is a better place because you are in it... I
love you with all my heart...

(Michael),... you are very smart... I know you see
something and know it can work... after all... you have
seen it work for other people... what you don't know is
other people did not learn to do it their first time either...
you see (Mommy and Daddy) do something it looks like

it is easy... well... you are right... it is easy... and (we)
had to learn to do it just like you are learning to do it...
it took practice... sometimes the harder something is...
the more practice it takes... the next time you go to do
something and it is not going the way you want it to...
stop... take a deep breath... think about it for a moment
until the answer comes to you... then pick it up again
and finish it... you may have to stop several times... and
that is okay... stop... take a deep breath... wait... then go
ahead and finish... you are smart... I know you know
the answer... you have to be patient with yourself... you
are smart.

It took me a little while to understand why Michael
was so frustrated. My affirmation must have been right,
because I only had to use this Pillow Talk once with
Michael. Within the week, his teacher commented that
he seemed calmer and more relaxed at school.

Reflection: As parents, we need to be empathetic.
Understanding the emotion is half the battle.
Sometimes saying "I see you are frustrated" lets the
child know that you understand the experience.

Based on the principles of *Parenting*
with Love and Logic: Teaching
Children Responsibility, by
Foster W. Cline and Jim Fay, I
would encourage letting your
children do things for themselves,
so they will learn through
their own experience. Let
them have their own failures
to learn by. At the same time,

keep things age-appropriate. They need to have more successes than failures to keep their spirit intact, so find the balance and be a helpful partner rather than an impatient "Let me do it" parent—or a "Just forget it" parent, as I had been.

perseverance

love

patience

Reading

Michael started in kindergarten at a Montessori program, which allowed him to learn at his own speed. For Michael, learning to read was not natural, and the Montessori program was not going to force him to read; after all, it would happen when it became important to him. I am okay with that. He is accelerated at his math and science skills. He also has a strong spirit and believes in himself. The Montessori Method had a very positive impact on who he is as an individual.

When Michael started the first grade at public school, we soon discovered he had not planned on learning to read. Before moving forward in public school, children must be able to complete certain tasks, and reading is one of them. Michael's first-grade teacher would send him home with books, and I would sit down to have him read them to me. Michael would assume all kinds of positions on the couch next to me, including upside-down and hanging over the edge. One Saturday morning, I asked Michael to come and read to me. He read one word and said, "I am hungry." I looked at the time, and it was legitimately lunch time. I told him, "Let's have lunch, and right after lunch you have to read before you get to do anything else." We had lunch and sat down to read again. We got into an argument because I asked him to start from the beginning and read the first word over again, and he wanted to start from the second word. I told him to go ahead and go to his room, and when he was ready to start from the beginning then he could come out.

A Half an hour went by and he did not come out. I went to his room and said, "Michael, I am wrong. You can come out and play. You do not have to learn to read if you do not want to. But I need you to know what kind of jobs people get when they do not learn how to read. (I then described some jobs.) You can make your choice, but I want you to know how it may turn out."

Michael came out of his room in less than a minute and said, "Okay, Mom, I am ready to read from the beginning." That night I gave the following affirmation:

Stay asleep (Michael), this is (Mommy).
Stay asleep (Michael), this is (Mommy).
Stay asleep (Michael), this is (Mommy).
Stay asleep (Michael), this is (Mommy).
Stay asleep (Michael), this is (Mommy).
Stay asleep (Michael), this is (Mommy).

(Michael), I love you... thank you for being in my life... I am the luckiest (mommy) in the world to have such a wonderful (son) as (Michael)... my heart is filled with joy and the world is a better place because you are in it... I love you with all my heart...

(Michael),... you are very smart... now that you have decided to learn to read... reading is going to be very easy for you... you go to school... learn from the teacher... the teacher will tell you what you need to know... we will practice at home at night... reading is very easy for you... it is easy for you to learn new things.

Reading is not totally logical. There are rules, but there are exceptions to almost all of them. We enrolled Michael into Sylvan Learning System, which had a methodical approach to reading that fit Michael's learning style. When Michael started first grade, he was reading at or below kindergarten level. By the end of the second trimester, Michael easily was reading at grade level and was taken out of the public schools special reading class. By the end of first grade, Michael's reading level was equal to the middle of second grade. He will even spend his allowance to buy books. None of this would have happened if Michael had not decided for himself that reading was important.

I reinforced Michael's reading by making it a rule that he had to read at least ten minutes before I would sing night-time songs. I remember coming home from a 14-hour shift and walking into Michael's room to kiss him. He asked me to sing. I asked if he had read yet. He said he had forgotten, and then he jumped up and grabbed a book and sat down and read to me.

Reflection: public schools simply are not designed to help all children learn at their own individual pace and in their own individual styles. It was extremely important we found a resource to help Michael learn according to his needs.

Reading Test

In the first grade, Michael was required to take a lot of oral reading comprehension tests. The people who were administering the tests said they felt that Michael understood the material, because when they asked him specific details he had the right answers for them. However, because of the nature of the test, they wanted him to volunteer the information when they asked him to retell the story, and he had not been doing that. I gave him the following affirmation:

Stay asleep (Michael), this is (Mommy).
Stay asleep (Michael), this is (Mommy).
Stay asleep (Michael), this is (Mommy).
Stay asleep (Michael), this is (Mommy).
Stay asleep (Michael), this is (Mommy).
Stay asleep (Michael), this is (Mommy).

(Michael), I love you... thank you for being in my life... I am the luckiest (mommy) in the world to have such a wonderful (son) as (Michael)... my heart is filled with joy and the world is a better place because you are in it... I love you with all my heart...

(Michael),... when your teachers ask you to tell them about the story... they are asking you to tell them everything you remember... so simply tell them everything from the

very beginning until the end... I know you know it...
so simply tell them everything about the story from
the beginning to the end.

It was such a simple Pillow Talk. The teachers had
already asked him to do the same thing, but this
worked.

Reflection: Use simple ideas. Remember, Michael had
been told what to do, but until I told him in Pillow
Talk, he did not produce the results the teachers were
looking for.

confidence

love

empowerment

WRITING

As you can imagine, a child who does not have very good reading skills also has challenges with writing. For Michael, it seemed that writing was a chore. His first-grade teacher recognized his wonderful verbal skills and was hopeful he could put his creative thoughts into writing. I spoke with Michael and asked him about writing. He said that he did not know what to say. That night in Pillow Talk I gave him the following affirmation:

Stay asleep (Michael), this is (Mommy).
Stay asleep (Michael), this is (Mommy).
Stay asleep (Michael), this is (Mommy).
Stay asleep (Michael), this is (Mommy).
Stay asleep (Michael), this is (Mommy).
Stay asleep (Michael), this is (Mommy).

(Michael), I love you... thank you for being in my life... I am the luckiest (mommy) in the world to have such a wonderful (son) as (Michael)... my heart is filled with joy and the world is a better place because you are in it... I love you with all my heart...

(Michael),... you are very smart... it is easy for you to learn new things... when the teacher asks you to write... and you don't know what to write... it is okay to write about nothing at all... start writing... "I don't know what I want to write about... so I am writing about not knowing what to write about... then before long I have written about not knowing what to write about"... then your teacher is happy because you have written something... you are lucky you are so smart.

Michael's teacher had immediate feedback. She said, "I don't know what it is, but Michael has suddenly taken off and really started to write."

Reflection: With the help of my family, I find ways to help Michael and Sarah understand the value of being able to write. When we take a vacation, I have them write a postcard to their schools and the grandparents, and then when they get back they get to share their experiences with their class and family. I also like them to write thank-you notes for presents they receive, and then the people who receive the thank-you notes are very good about reinforcing how appreciative they are to receive acknowledgment of their gifts.

clarity

love

independence

FORGIVENESS

Michael at age seven kept pestering Sarah without provocation. Most parents raising more than one child at home can relate to the seeming accident of messing up the dollhouse or bumping into a little sister in the middle of an art project: that sibling rivalry stuff, you know. Whenever I asked Michael why he was doing that, he would say it was an accident. But it was obvious to me there was some hostility. About once a month, Michael would let me know of something Sarah had done as a baby or a toddler. I realized he was having difficulty forgiving her. It was obvious to me most of the things Sarah had done were just natural curiosity and nothing really mean, but to Michael they were insulting. It seemed beyond his emotional skills to see the difference, and he appeared to have no tolerance for either one.

Stay asleep (Michael), this is (Mommy).
Stay asleep (Michael), this is (Mommy).
Stay asleep (Michael), this is (Mommy).
Stay asleep (Michael), this is (Mommy).
Stay asleep (Michael), this is (Mommy).
Stay asleep (Michael), this is (Mommy).

(Michael), I love you... thank you for being in my life... I am the luckiest (mommy) in the world to have such a wonderful (son) as (Michael)... my heart is filled with joy and the world is a better place because you are in it... I love you with all my heart...

(Michael),... forgiving is very important for you... when you hold onto your anger... it makes your heart smaller... have you ever seen a person who seems mad all the time?... that is a person who has not learned to forgive... forgiving does not mean forgetting... if someone does something bad to hurt you... or something mean... it does not mean you have to forget it happened... it does not mean that person has to be your friend... it does mean that you no longer feel the anger of the unfairness... so when someone does something unfair... instead of getting angry... you may start to ask, "What did I learn from this to make my life better?"... (this is especially true when it comes to Sarah... she is your sister... you love her... there may be no one person in your life you will know longer than you will know and love Sarah)... it is important for you to forgive (her)... learn the lesson from the unfair experience... (the lesson God and Jesus would want you to learn)... (how would God want you to respond?)... perhaps... thank the person you are angry with... and bless that person for the new lesson you have gained in your life... forgiving is important... I love you.

(Personalize your own Pillow Talk to correspond to your family's belief system because those are the values your children are familiar with, and they are consistent with their environment.)

Michael and Sarah have played very well together for many years. They seem like best friends. Since I had this Pillow Talk with Michael, he reduced his sibling incidents by more than half. Now he seems to do most of his big-brother acting-out more out of boredom, to shake things up, than just to even the score. He is playful about it and follows it up with a "Let's do... " instead of pretending it is an accident and that he has absolutely no idea how something like that could have happened.

In the middle of this affirmation, I included a recent experience Michael had gone through. He was proud of his allowance money and was showing it to a girl a few years older. She said she needed something for school and asked to look at the ten-dollar bill. Michael gave it to her. She said she would give it back if he gave her his five. So he did. She walked off with his five-dollar bill. Michael was already a little okay with what had happened because she had said she needed the money, and he was happy to help. But he also said he did not know if he should have trusted her, because there was something about her that made him think she was probably not being truthful. Mark and I discussed the situation with both Michael and Sarah and explained there are a few people out in the world who will take advantage of people, even children. We explained that it was important not to show people your money and not to even talk about having money. We told Michael that he was probably lucky to learn that lesson at such a young age.

I added this part to the middle of the above affirmation to help Michael relate to what I mean when I talk about forgiveness:

> ... (like that little girl who took your money... forgiveness does not mean you have to have her as a friend or play with her... it does mean when you think about her you are no longer mad... in fact... you may want to thank her for giving you a life lesson... she taught you that you don't show your money to people... and you don't talk about how much money you have)...

Reflection: Forgiveness is one of my life lessons. As a critical care nurse, I know how short life is. I have spent the last few years in a quest to learn what forgiveness means to me. I have my faults. I have learned that, as much as I need to forgive other people's actions, I also have to forgive mine. Now, under my own understanding of forgiveness, I have blessed the lessons learned, and I am a much better person than I ever was. When I find myself mad about something, I attempt to forgive it and move on. Some things are going to be harder than others, and I would recommend getting professional help if that is what it takes to start moving life forward again.

Consider reading the book *The Precious Present*, by Spencer Johnson, M.D., to understand what I mean. The book offers a simple metaphor about moving forward in life by living in the minute, not in the past or the future. It is one of my favorites.

forgiveness

growth

generosity

SUNBURN

At age seven, Michael had gone swimming with his summer-school class. Michael is fair-skinned and does not tolerate sun well. He had applied sunscreen SPF 30, but he was still not able to handle the noonday sun. When I came home from a 14-hour shift, I noticed he had a sunburn that was obviously going to blister. I applied aloe vera lotion and told Michael to go ahead and start talking to his body and letting it know he was no longer in the sun, so his skin no longer had to stay hot; in fact his skin was protected under his shirt and it was cool and dark.

Michael has good luck with talking to his body in this fashion, and he started to feel immediate relief. As he went to bed, I gave him the following Pillow Talk:

Stay asleep (Michael), this is (Mommy).
Stay asleep (Michael), this is (Mommy).
Stay asleep (Michael), this is (Mommy).
Stay asleep (Michael), this is (Mommy).
Stay asleep (Michael), this is (Mommy).
Stay asleep (Michael), this is (Mommy).

(Michael), I love you... thank you for being in my life...
I am the luckiest (mommy) in the world to have such a
wonderful (son) as (Michael)... my heart is filled with joy
and the world is a better place because you are in it... I
love you with all my heart...

(Michael),... let your body know that it is cool and safe...
it is no longer in the sun... so it is cool and safe... the

burn goes away... your skin is cool and safe... it is night-time and it is cool and safe... it no longer needs to burn... the heat leaves the skin... it is cool and safe.

The next day Michael's sunburn was nearly gone. He had minimal peeling of his shoulders. I understand the aloe vera helped in reducing his burn, but the improvement went beyond the effects of the lotion.

I have taught Michael to listen to his body and it will talk to him. I explain that it is not in a voice like mine, but in the way a body talks. When it is hungry, he may notice a change in his body such as feeling just a little weak, possibly a gnawing in his stomach, etc. He is getting used to the signals it gives him. Often when he asks a question about his body, I will ask him, "What do you think?" He will search within and come up with amazing answers. I have also taught him he can tell his body his own affirmations, as I did in the example of the sunburn.

Reflection: I have noticed in my experience as a critical care nurse it is easy for people to recognize that others can make themselves "sick with worry." I have witnessed numerous people who have had a technically good surgery who have failed to recover because of a poor mindset.

It does seem to be more challenging for people to accept that with positive affirmations they can focus themselves well. This is one of the greatest lessons that Anthony Robbins, Napoleon Hill, and Linda Gentry helped me to learn. To simplify the concept: You visualize the outcome, and then make it real in your mind.

To take full advantage of positive affirmations for yourself, visualize the positive outcome right before you go to sleep, and then once again as you awaken in the morning. Start taking the action toward making the desired outcome a reality. Attach emotion to your outcome. The more excitement you evoke when you visualize your outcome, the greater the outcome. When you use Pillow Talk, you are taking advantage of the night-time visualization with your children.

Conclusion of Part One

I hope you have found my examples helpful. If you have not read them all, I encourage you to go back and read the ones you missed. I have modeled helpful ideas and included my reflections to assist you in creating your own affirmations. Remember, you are telling your children the same things you would tell them if they were awake; however, you are taking advantage of their having their waking senses turned off. In Part Two, I will discuss how to create your own Pillow Talk.

Part Two: Create Your Own Affirmations

Hopefully your mind is reeling with wonderful ideas of how you are going to use Pillow Talk with your children, and you are as excited as I was when my ideas came rushing to me for the first time as you learn from my examples, lessons, and mistakes from Part One. In Part Two, I will give you ideas about how to build your own affirmations. First, though, I would like to get the topic of control out into the open.

Can I control my children?

It seems when they are asleep, just as when they are awake, my children still resist suggestions that go against their natural inclinations. I attempted to Pillow Talk my children into keeping their toys picked up and put away. I used all kinds of angles. It did not work to any degree I was hoping for. It simply was not in their nature to be that neat at this age.

Sarah provides another example of how children cannot be controlled with Pillow Talk. Getting Sarah to brush her teeth was ridiculous. For her, brushing her teeth meant she was going to go to bed, and she did not want to miss out on anything. I used Pillow Talk. I used discipline. We even started to take away the privilege of having sugar treats the next day, which was the most motivating of the above. Then I told her if she had her teeth brushed and night-time clothes on by nine o'clock, she would earn one video minute. She now runs to the bathroom at night-time to get her teeth brushed by nine o'clock.

I designed a plan that works well for our family. I let the kids earn video and computer minutes by doing chores. Each chore has a video/computer minute value. They can only play videos or computer games at home using the minutes they have accumulated.

Where do the words come from?

Listen to your heart and let the words flow with the intense love you feel. Be loving in the words you choose and in your tone of voice.

Before formulating many of my affirmations, I like to watch my children's behavior and use my motherly intuition to understand the motives behind their actions.

Trust your instincts and listen to your children. Michael is old enough that I can ask him questions to narrow down what I think his motive is.

Our conversation may go like this:

Me: Michael, why do you think that happened?
Michael: I don't know.
Me: But if you did know, why would you think that happened?
Michael: I told you I don't know.
Me: I know you don't know, but if you did know?
Michael: Well... (followed by his answer).

This is a fascinating technique. You can ask the question "But if you did know" a lot of times, followed up with "Of course you don't know, but if you did know." Although it can get very annoying to the person you are doing it to, it can really work. The source of their annoyance is usually not the person asking the question, but rather their own struggle to find the answer.

A great place for you to find positive affirmations is within your religious beliefs and books. Also, Louise L. Hay in her book *You Can Heal Your Life* offers beautifully stated affirmations. Perhaps you can even use affirmations from greeting cards. Once you start looking, you may find them almost anywhere.

How specific should I be?

In the very first sentence of your affirmation, state the exact outcome you desire. Be specific. In each sentence that follows, support the thought and idea of the first sentence. For instance, I tell Sarah she is beautiful. Then I support the sentence by defining beauty according to my beliefs and pointing out the actions she takes that agree with my definition. "Sarah, you are beautiful... beautiful is not what you look like... beauty is who you are... beauty is what you do... and because you are kind and loving... you are beautiful."

Are there particular words or phrases you recommend?

Speak in absolutes. Speaking in absolutes is essential to any good affirmation. I want to emphasize this point: It means saying what the goal is. A great way to achieve behavior modification is by creating only the pictures and

feelings that are needed. For example, from Part One, when I was giving Sarah her affirmation on getting her haircut, I focused on the behavior I wanted her to have. Instead of telling her to stop running around the hair salon, I suggested she sit in the chair and Katie would instruct her. The subconscious mind works in the same fashion.

Use the word "because." Using the word "because" creates a cause and effect. In other words, when your children have a specific behavior, they are going to get results. "When you study your assignment, you are going to do better at school, because you are learning what the teacher expects you to know from your school work."

Use the words "before now." This is important when there is a transition going on. Perhaps there was negative behavior of overeating, and it is a challenge for your children's self-image to see themselves as healthy, because they look in the mirror and see only their reflection. If the goal is weight loss, you need to help them move past the body image and visualize their true self: someone who now is committed to taking care of their body. They must visualize a new image of health. They need to develop a new image of their body as it will look once they reach their goal. Using the words "before now" may ease this contradiction. Use the words "before now" in a way that empowers: "Before now, you may not have taken care of yourself in a loving and healthy manner, but now see yourself as a person who loves your body, and takes care of yourself by eating healthy, nutritious foods; drinking life-giving, energizing water; and exercising (by walking) every day." Create a visual image of the desired body, how clothes are going to fit, and the new things your child will be able to experience with a healthier body. Set achievable goals. Consult with the pediatrician or nutritionist for a realistic and healthy diet and weight-loss plan.

Are there particular words or phrases to avoid?

Avoid the words "no" and "not." Think of it this way: Right now, don't think of your favorite snack, no matter what. Don't imagine what your favorite snack tastes like, what it looks like, or especially how yummy it smells when it is fixed exactly the way you love it. Wow, what happened

to your thoughts? For most of us, it is nearly impossible not to think of our favorite snack. Perhaps you are even thinking of how to get it now as you are reading, even though you were told not to think about it at all.

Here is a typical example of how we fall into this trap. Imagine for a moment that your child is running next to the pool. It is common to yell, "Don't run." Instead, tell your children the behavior that will help keep them safe. Tell them to "walk." There is a difference. The subconscious mind has a hard time processing the words "no" and "not."

When my children were young and learning the meaning of words, I rarely used the word "no." Instead I would use the word "danger" or "stop." They quickly learned to halt in their tracks when they heard the word "danger." They knew it meant "ouch" for them, and the word "stop" meant I disapproved of what they were doing.

Avoid the phrase "you will." For instance, "You will be strong" is a weak statement. The word "will" has no time frame or commitment to it. Will you be strong next week or in five years? Who is to know? Instead, "You are strong and becoming stronger because you run every day and take care of your body by eating healthy, energy-giving foods and drinking life-giving water." In this sentence, you are already strong and making yourself stronger by specific activities.

Avoid the phrase "you want to." The word "want" leaves you in a state of wanting. "Want" rarely succeeds. "You want to be the best soccer player ever." Sure, we all want a lot of things, but we have to take action to achieve them. Instead, "You are a great soccer player, and you are getting better all the time. To be the best soccer player you have to practice with your coach to do the drills and exercise, and take care of your body by eating healthy, energizing foods and drinking life-giving water."

Avoid the phrase "try to." "Try" is a very weak word. "You try to get your homework done on time." "Try" implies failure. "Yes, I tried, but I just could not do it," and "I tried my hardest." Instead, "You get your homework done, because you know it is important to do well in school. When you get your homework done, you feel good about yourself, because it feels good to complete your assignment, and you know you can do anything."

Leave out the word "but." This can be a real challenge. Most of us are used to using the word "but" and never think about how it negates every word in front of it. "I know you are nice, but other people would recognize how nice you are if you used your good manners all of the time." Instead use the word "and." Say, "I know you are nice, and other people recognize how nice you are when you use your good manners all of the time."

In this sentence, the word "and" allows the first part of the sentence to still be true.

Leave out the word "just." The word belittles the thought that goes with it. "You could get the work done if you just put your mind to it." In this example, you need to listen to why your children feel they have not been able to get the work done. Is there a roadblock your parental wisdom could help them redefine or take down? For example, do their feet hurt every time they jump? Is there someone they don't like to be around? Help discover the hurdle that is keeping them from completing the work. There may be times they need motivation, and you can help them find the motivation using your wonderful parenting techniques.

Leave out the word "should." The word "should" has no absolute, and it typically sounds nagging. "You should wear your seatbelt every time you ride in the car." Instead say, "Every time you ride in the car, wear your seat belt to keep yourself safe."

Wow! A lot of your examples are for talking to your children while they are awake. Why is that?

Good words work. You can improve your communication in all parts of your life by using the guidelines for words and phrases to use and avoid described in the above examples.

Please also understand these examples are not limited to the words listed above. Avoid replacing negative words or statements with others that have similar meanings, or implying them with your tone of voice or body language. If your tone reflects the thought "Just get up and do it," have you really listened to your child? The tone of our words and the body language in which we speak carry more significance than the words themselves. That is another reason why Pillow Talk works: It turns off the nonverbal communication with your children, so they are listening to your words.

Should I write a practice Pillow Talk?

Yes, please do. Read it over to make certain the very first sentence is the desired outcome or behavior. Then each following sentence needs to support that thought. Review each sentence for the words to use and the words to avoid. Look at each sentence and evaluate it as if it

were five years from now, and then ten years from now, and see whether the statement is still true. You may need to add an age-appropriate out—as, for example, when I tell Sarah, "For now only Katie cuts you hair... you may decide when you get older...."

Make changes as needed to create a Pillow Talk from love. One of my favorite questions—and I say it to myself before I get started—is one I learned from Neale Donald Walsch: "What would love say now?" If it is not a thought from love, leave it out.

In creating your Pillow Talk, find the words that will allow the desired behavior to grow most naturally from the child's personality. Avoid demands; be persuasive and clever. I think of it as taking the dictator out of the conversation. For example, when Michael did not want to learn to read, I told him he did not have to. In that moment I removed the battle of authority and enticed him to make his own decision. We had no further conflict, because he made his own decision to learn to read based on the information I shared with him on how his life might turn out if he never learned. He realized the downside of his prior decision and was allowed to make the right decision based on his own values. The experience left him feeling not defeated but informed.

Is age a factor?

I was told that affirmations have the greatest effect with children younger than seven. The logic behind this theory is that most people have not developed their reasoning until then, and once they have reached that milestone they will be less open to suggestion. However,

I am not certain this theory has ever been proven. I do know self-directed affirmations work on adults. It also seems to make sense that infants could benefit from a loving, nurturing statement from either parent. Just by the tones of our voices we project the love we have in our hearts. Because we believe in our own words, we connect ourselves to our children, creating a synergistic communication.

Because I started using Pillow Talk with Sarah and Michael at such an early age, they will probably continue to accept it from me as part of our family routine. Michael, at age eight, remains receptive. However, Michael is more likely than Sarah to open his eyes when I am talking to him, and he just watches me quietly. He calls it "giving me my praises."

If you have older children, consider sitting down and speaking with them about Pillow Talk before you even start. Explain that you will be coming to talk to them while they are asleep and you are going to be using words of love and encouragement, and explain your motives. (They are specific to you, so find your own words.) Then, get their permission; ask if that would be okay with them. You might explain that the first couple of times it might wake them up, and after a few nights it will be easy to drift back to sleep. Better yet, an older child may want to help work with you on your combined goals and the words to use during their Pillow Talk.

Compounding an idea becomes more important as children age and move into the adult mind. They have developed more roadblocks along the way. Start your idea with the very specific outcome you desire. Every sentence afterwards becomes a supporting sentence. With adults it is thought that you need to repeat the specific outcome at least 15 times or more.

Should both parents get involved?

Yes, each parent brings a different aspect of balance to their children. I believe Sarah and Michael respond differently to my Pillow Talks compared to Mark's. There are going to be some things they find more believable from Mark than from me. For example, because I screamed so terribly when Sarah was being stung by the wasp, the "Bugs" Pillow Talk seemed more credible coming from Mark—although it was important for me to work with Sarah on it, too, because I did overreact. I needed to help her understand that I also have respect for bugs.

How often should I do Pillow Talk?

Pillow Talk as often as you like. I skip several nights, and even weeks. It is really up to you.

I was told you have to talk to them right at the moment they fall asleep. Is this true?

That works very well, but because of my work hours I am often not home when my children go to bed. I have found that by lightly stroking their faces or caressing their hands or shoulders and saying their names, I do lighten their sleep cycle. Just in case, as with Sarah getting her teeth pulled or her hair cut, I will go to their room for a couple nights prior to an event to give them affirmations.

How long should it be?

Keep it short. Children move through their sleep cycles quickly. Even though you lighten their sleep by touching them lightly and saying their names, you typically want to keep the entire Pillow Talk between about half a minute and one minute.

Can I use different words?

Obviously a newborn does not have language skills, and it seems reasonable that talking in a loving fashion helps build a bond. Go ahead and use the words and concepts you feel your children will understand at their current age. Some people believe children "grow" into the words: If they do not understand what you are saying now, they may understand later as they develop emotionally, and the thoughts will be in their subconscious ready for them to use.

Whatever words you choose, keep it simple.

How can I tell whether it is working?

When I Pillow Talk to my children, Sarah's breathing changes, and Michael turns his body toward my voice. There have even been times when Michael's head would nod as I was talking to him.

I like to evaluate the results from the changes in behavior, as shown in my examples in Part One. If a child was struggling with something before the Pillow Talk, is she still struggling with it afterwards? If so, is it because she was in too deep a sleep? Was the affirmation inconsistent with the child's self-belief? Sometimes the motivation behind a child's behavior is not immediately apparent, and parents may have to observe the situation awhile longer before they discover the right affirmation for the child's needs.

The success of Pillow Talk will be assisted by your great parenting techniques. You can reinforce your affirmations during the daytime by giving your children positive feedback for desired behaviors. You get to reinforce your choice of words with your actions.

What if my child is having disturbing behavior?

Pillow Talk cannot substitute for professional help. Please use this technique only to bring nurturing to your children's lives and to supplement the skills you already have. You may want to consult with your pediatrician before you begin using or creating your own Pillow Talk affirmations.

Get professional help if your child displays behaviors that are disturbing or harmful.

What were the names of the resources you listed?

Dr. Becky Bailey, *Conscious Discipline*
Foster W. Cline and Jim Fay, *Parenting with Love and Logic: Teaching Children Responsibility*
Walt Disney Pictures, *The Incredibles*
Linda Gentry, MIH, Warrensburg, MO, my mentor
Napoleon Hill, *Think and Grow Rich*
Spencer Johnson, M.D., *The One Minute Mother*
Spencer Johnson, M.D., *The Precious Present*
Anthony Robbins, "Unleash the Power Within" – conference

A Note from the Author

Thank you for your time! I am Nancy Beck, a registered nurse with a Bachelor of Science degree in nursing from the University of Missouri–Columbia and 21 years' experience as a critical care nurse. This book grew out of what I have learned from the many self-development courses I have taken over the years in an effort to improve my life and my nursing skills. Through Mastery University with Anthony Robbins, I was introduced to the power of words and their effect on the body and mind. From the lessons learned in this training, I had to turn away from the concept that things just happen to us, and that we really are just victims of our circumstances. A seed was planted, and my reaction to life had to change. I was not fully ready. Next I studied Napoleon Hill's *Think and Grow Rich*. I had a new level of understanding the power of language and thought, which enabled me to start taking control of my body and mind by choosing the proper words. I then took training from my mentor Linda Gentry specifically about the effect of words on the subconscious mind, and how to use them to bring results to my body and to help people around me with my new skills. These experiences allowed me to bring the information of *Pillow Talk* to you.

I hope that you get profound results using Pillow Talk with your children. It is truly simple. May you and your family be blessed with much happiness, and your children grow with strong and healthy spirits.

With love,
Nancy Beck

Author · Nancy Beck